BLOOD EARTH AND

a year in the life of a
casual agricultural labourer

by James Crowden

with a foreword by John Fowles

Parrett Press, Martock
1991

First published in October 1991
by the Parrett Press, Martock, Somerset.
© James Crowden, 1991
All rights reserved.
A CIP record for this book is
available from the British Library.
ISBN 1-872723-02-0
Grateful acknowledgement is made
to South West Arts for a grant
towards the cost of publication.

WITH THE ASSISTANCE OF

SOUTH WEST ARTS

New

CONTENTS

ACKNOWLEDGEMENTS

As far as writing is concerned, I have often worked totally alone over the last ten years, but recently I have sought the opinion and comments of others, and their reactions which were in the main positive, have convinced me that the poetry was worth publishing.

Here I would like to thank John Fowles, Seamus Heaney, John Crook, Christopher Reid, Winston Graham, Ingrid Squirrell, Andy Baker, Mark Roper, Elinor Bagenal, John Thorley, Paddy Ashdown, Sir Richard Body, Chris Chapman, Nick Purcell, David Burnett, Julian Temperley, Ann Hodgson, Graham Crowden, Schuyler Jones, Peter Montagnon, Mike Eatough, Robert Tilleard, Janet and Geoffrey Jenkins, Audrey Hall, Peter Irving, Barney Rosedale, John and Simon Eastwood, Karen Etherington, George Wright, Mike Mouland, Mary Carstairs, Evelyn Body, Michael Donovan alias Nathaniel of Wessex, and many others.

Your help and encouragement in even the smallest matters has been tremendous. Thank you.

For initial finance I am indebted to my father, whose support and encouragement have been much appreciated over the years.

I must mention also Nicholas Sloan of the Parrett Press, whose dedication to good printing has given the book an added dimension that it would not have possessed had it gone through the normal publishing channels.

Most important of all, my wife Olivia in between making her sculpture has helped endlessly, reading countless drafts. Her criticism is always sharp and perceptive, and has had an edge to it that is always refreshing. And last but not least my daughter Nell, aged 5, who has throughout her life seen everything and responded to it enthusiastically in a way which was spontaneous and completely natural. To be able to see and experience all these things first hand in childhood must be wonderful.

FOREWORD

James Crowden was born in Plymouth in 1954 and brought up on the edge of Dartmoor. We like to think that those who portray the simple life must have led very simple ones themselves. In James' case that is not quite right. Observant, poetic and expressive agricultural labourers have never been the rule: John Clare is an exception that proves it. In fact James studied civil engineering at Bristol and (no surprise to anyone who reads this book carefully) anthropology at Oxford. He was briefly in the Army, intending it as a permanent career, but left it in 1976. He was also a mountaineer and has travelled widely in places as far apart as Afghanistan and the Yukon, Eastern Turkey, Ladakh and the Outer Hebrides.

But for the last decade—of which this book is a reflection—he has been returning to his roots, indeed all our roots, and has earned his living from shearing, night-lambing, cider-making and a woodman's varied tasks. Married, he now lives in Winsham in Somerset, just north of the border with West Dorset. What immediately struck me about this book was how well it recorded very humble-seeming, if once essential and ubiquitous, forms of labour. They are ones, though we may not fully accept and realise it, that lie deep in almost all our archetypal selves. Other writers —Ted Hughes and John Stuart Collis spring to mind—have also returned to that knowledge of ancient craft, that intimacy with nature, and have explored its peasant character, its bloodymindedness and wisely enduring resonances.

James Crowden's 'writings' (the term was suggested by Seamus Heaney, admiring, but not quite content with 'poems') are a precious and impressive evocation of that very ancient way of life. It is one that lies, though more than half forgotten, in the national bloodstream. I have always pitied the young and urbanised, from whose transistorised and media-ridden universe, that world has so largely disappeared. Life is more than a video game in the back room of a pub. Here is a vividly close memory of what they have missed.

John Fowles

INTRODUCTION

Most of the material for *Blood Earth & Medicine* has been gathered over the last ten years in Dorset and Somerset, with occasional forays over the border into Devon and Wiltshire, an area approximating to the old kingdom of Wessex. I wanted to live life in the raw, and so in a sense my lifestyle was dictated by the nature of the land, as well as a few chance encounters. The time which I had spent abroad in mountainous regions had impressed upon me the fundamental importance of agriculture and the deep relationship that should naturally exist between people and the land.

Very quickly I came to realise that farming in the affluent West had somehow got ahead of itself in ways which were not entirely beneficial, and so I preferred to work alongside those people who were less willing to keep pace with the hectic precision of modern methods, for they had unwittingly preserved an essential backwater in a countryside that is all too often eroded and misunderstood. Over the years I came to appreciate the importance of their work, their craft, their intuition and the things that they were trying to say but left unsaid.

At first sight poetry might seem to be a strange medium in which to record my observations, but it has the advantages of precision & immediacy that are somehow lacking in a more objective approach. For a short while I used a tape-recorder, and for this small project I was given a grant of £150 by the Shaftesbury and Gillingham Agricultural Society. Although the recordings were good, I was not quite getting what I wanted. What I sought to record was far more subtle. Gossip and reminiscence although valuable to the local historian, was not my primary aim. What interested me was the work and the way in which it influenced people's lives & their thinking. Farming has changed out of all proportion in the last 40 years, and mechanisation, although leading to greater efficiency, has taken a fair chunk out of people's knowledge and intuition. The residue of eight thousand years of farming I decided did not lie so much in a tractor manual as in the unspoken attitudes of certain shepherds and casual labourers, who perhaps more than any other group represent the patterns of agriculture before the Enclosure

Acts. These combined with incomers & second homes have done more to change village structure than the Norman Conquest.

Be that as it may, my intention was to produce something that was a combination of alternative anthropology and literature. No easy task, and yet by using the eye of one and the ear of the other I have tried to bridge the gap, and have learnt much from the poetry of the East, in particular from Basho, who lived in Japan 1644-94. His *haiku* and travel sketches are well known, and something of his perception and depth of observation have haunted me. A well known saying of his runs like this:

> *Go to the pine tree if you want to learn about the pine, or to the bamboo stalk if you want to learn about the bamboo.*
> And in so doing you must leave your own preoccupation with yourself. You should let your mind enter the object until there comes a point when they are indistinguishable, and you share the same feelings. Only then will a poem emerge of its own accord. If the feeling is unnatural and the opposites arise, then the poem is not a true poem. You should let the mind and the object become one. Pure description is not enough.

Perhaps without quite realising what I was doing at first, I applied the essence of this advice not just to one object but to a whole group of people. What emerged may well have certain resonances that will only become apparent in years to come. The writing therefore works on several levels, and the reader should be prepared to let the images work on their own.

What may seem simple and innocuous to a city dweller has deep meaning for those that never left the country.

Also, I feel in a sense that the work could be seen as a response to the *koan* of *The Waste Land*, though this only occured to me long after I had finished writing it. So much has been written on *The Waste Land*, and so much of it goes round in circles, that it seems much simpler just to regard the whole work as a question and not an answer. For Eliot the answer was obviously contained in *Four Quartets*, but that was predominantly a Christian answer.

Blood Earth & Medicine has none of Eliot's copious erudition, the truths are instinctive and earthy, not academic, but *The Waste Land* was his desert, and anyone who has seriously tackled *koans* on a strict Zen retreat knows what the desert is. Every year I shear a small flock of sheep in East Coker, within a stone's throw of the church where Eliot's ashes are buried, and as I do so, I feel as though I am in touch with a tradition that he perhaps only guessed at, and which, if he had really let himself go, would have given him ultimately in life what he sought in death.

These are only my own thoughts, and the reader can make his or her judgement, if indeed a judgement is needed. The answer is therefore an agricultural and rural answer and one which could only have come from the land, which to my way of thinking is far from waste, though when I look at rough patches of 'set-aside' I begin to wonder. There may well be other answers, but for the moment, living as I do in the West Country, the one which has emerged will have to do.

All of culture is in a sense an answer to the three basic *koans*: Where have we come from? What are we? Where are we going? Which curiously enough is the title of one of Gaugin's most extraordinary paintings. It is twelve feet wide, and he painted it just before he tried to commit suicide. Everybody tries to answer these questions in their lifetime even if they are not consciously aware of it. It is simply an expression of man's natural curiosity. Ironically in the bottom left hand corner of the picture is a white bird symbolising the futility of words.

Blood Earth & Medicine is therefore dedicated to all farm labourers past and present, whose silence and reticence are all about us, and in particular those with whom I came in close contact. Quite a few are mentioned in the notes, and some are no longer with us. I was particularly sad to read in the paper last week of the death of one Frederick Chubb, known to his friends simply as 'Ikey'. He was a free spirit living rough and ready in the hills between Stoke Abbot and Beaminster. Aged 66, he was killed by a tractor which rolled over on top of him while he was harrowing. Steep ground is never easy at the best of times. Scruffy, untidy and smelling of snuff, he would go out rabbiting, catching moles & doing people's gardens. He couldn't read or write and even tried to get his pension a year or two early because he wasn't quite sure how old he was. He used to catch sheep for us and sing songs in the shearing shed. His lurcher I am told sat by the tractor for 24 hours until his absence was noticed.

James Crowden
8th May 1991

BLOOD EARTH AND MEDICINE

I HURDLEMAKING AND OLD MEN

Keen see how the sparhook dances
Glints like a fish in water
Scurrying upstream as it twists and turns.
Deftly the fine blade cleaves the hazel
Chasing each hidden bend
Grain rippling the same easy knack
Canny and sure of its subtle purpose.

To be alone, that is the secret
When the year is drawing to an end
To feel at home in the leaves
To feel the pulse of nature quietening down
Hermitlike in the depths of the coppice,
Surrounded and swallowed up by shavings.

And when the splitting is done and enough are gathered
The same stout fingers begin once more
To weave their ancient tapestry,
Coaxing and bending
Till the cleft rods rift and ride
Gleaming in curves like waves
Bucking and twisting
Through the silver bark of their flecked sea
A hurdle empowered by calloused hands,
Wrestling backwards and forwards
As if rowing a small coracle to a distant shore.

Pausing for a second, inquisitive and curious
Like a wild animal in the dappled light
The hurdlemaker listens to the coppice
Charting the silence, gauging its depth
As if his very life depended on it.

And when no one's looking, he slips the silence
Into the pocket of his battered tweed jacket
And takes it home, as you would
A rounded pebble that had caught your eye.

Look—a charcoal burner's pit

                  Sunlight glistening on silage bags
                  Larch turning

Dried grass
The smell of apples
Orchards

                  Coming home in droves
                  Sheep and mangolds

Geese flying overhead
The first stars
Woodsmoke

                  Dew on an autumn crocus
                  Timber seasoning

Voices in the woodshed
Leaves of Virginia creeper

                  Sawdust and cider presses
                  Bullocks' breath
                  The first frost

Teazles—so sharp and prickly
Behind the muckspreader,
Full moon rising

                  Caught at it
                  Two spiders in the bath

Old men shake their heads
And mutter under their breath...
Old men of the village
Like Incas, they stand and stare
Locked in cobbled silence
Their dry stone walls, time withered
And slipping through their gnarled hands
Fingers that once held the reins
Of strong horses, caressed them
And coaxed them home
Along the last painful furrow
Now clutch sticks
And cloudy glasses of rat's piss.

Hawking, they clear their throats
Spit out memories
Of large trees, bad winters
Mizzling wages.

Sudden death in the dan-dan.

Yoked to the land
Generations of wet feet went before you
Feet that could not escape the drudgery
Of open fields in winter
The harsh law: one for the rich
                    one for the poor.

Their ancestors created what you see
The earth tamed, ordered, nurtured.

Pushing up daisies, they could not even afford
Stones to mark their graves,
Only a slight hummock in the evening light.

Stubborn, diffuse, untidy
Only a handful left
These are the earth's true descendants
Who struggled to live
                    to stay alive.

Work alongside them, though they say little
Learn from them before it is too late.

II KITE HILL COPPICE

Always in winter, we are lighting fires
Underneath old tractors. Straw and oily rags
Coaxing them into life, flames licking
Up the blue belly, loosening the sump oil.
A burnt offering, a war horse
Fired up and ready to go.

Strange the yellow light through the trees,
The cold mist, the freezing fog
Rising off the river far below
Swirling like steam...

Fire and earth, ice and hoar frost

Like scraps of parchment
Our skin sticks to the steering wheel.

Keen see how the north-east wind knifes us,
Tears at our clothing, rough torn jackets
Torn on barbed wire and not yet mended.
This is winter boys, sharp as a razor.
Fell, thin, haul and extract
The harsh bark of chainsaws fills the valley.

Canny time and time again, gauging the ground
Slipping and slithering over hidden roots
Trailer load after trailer load
More than once, plunging down the wood
Out of control, the tractor
Nosediving for the fence.

Gears slip
   Tyres spin
      The rending crash
As metal breaks
   And judders to a halt.

Slowly the prolonged frost
Heaves the crumbling chalk
And deer come out of the woods
Bold and hungry, pawing the ground
Searching for grass and moss
The young shoots of winter corn.

Swift shadows, fleeting and curious.

Hard graft this living by one's hands
The spinning blade, the invisible teeth
Only inches away, the haze blurred and humming
The singing bird, forever pushing into the sawbench
Log after log, ton after ton, week after week
Endless cordwood, neatly stacked.

Hard graft this living by one's hands
The handle of the axe descending
Time after time, the sudden crack
As grain splits and yields its inner fragrance
Naked and sappy, a mountain of sawdust,
And not a jot does the eye's grasp wander.

Only at dusk does the silence return to the forest
Quivering and vital, as men go home
Returning to the firelight, a sense of knowing
Of having been there before.

More snow in the offing
Winter, winter, a season much maligned
For it hath in its grasp
Many beauties undefined:
The strength of the north east wind begins to tell.

III THE SMALL FARMER

Everything is just as it is.
Fences, ditches, crooked gates
Rime on windows, frozen taps
Feeding troughs full of snow
The cat half asleep in the barn
Dogs barking, the smell of cooking.

There, on the small, the poor farms
Live the true farmers and their wives
Scratching the soil and scraping their yards.
They live close to the land, feel its grasp
Claw deeper and deeper, solid and stubborn
Their obedience to the earth, firmly embedded
Under their fingernails, ingrained in the skin
Hidden in the teapot.

Boots, stick, dog
Slowly, carefully they patrol the fields
Peering into hedgerows.
Eyes and ears cocked.

Always in the country
People look at you straight on
And then sideways, when you're not looking
Just to be sure.

Sluggish and waiting
Nudging and swelling their way forward
Cows stand, ripe and firm outside the dairy
Vast their queuing udders,
Cubicle by cubicle, relief at last
Suction and a bit of grub.

Pulsing above their heads
In glass pipes and bottles
The doorstep gallons
Shunted round the county.

Long the winter—long the barn
Straw laden, slow and dark
Bound and trodden in by heavy hooves
The firmament rank and heady in its hibernation.
Beef cattle steam and heave their dung
Gutters leak and pigs squeal
Calves suck and cows piss in the sunlight.

A time for mucking out and a time for ploughing
A time for sowing and a time for harrowing.

Winter passes but still the grass does not grow.

Cold unexpected winds, maddened gusts
That drive the empty fertiliser bags
Around the yard, rattle roofs and doors
While half the world away, safe inside
His gentleman's residence, the wealthy farmer
Plans his shoot, and with a generous wave of his glass
Invites the local dignitaries to wine and dine.

Slowly the slurry gets on the move
Gargantuan containers, that guzzle up
The winter's froth, and spread it on the land
In fountains, gurgling voluptuously
Vomited over hedges, and on the roads
Slippery too.

Spring is definitely on the way
So they say.

IV TREE PLANTING

To start and start again, that is the secret

Even woodmen turn the soil over
In the wake of the burning brush.
Bonfire upon bonfire, clearing the slopes
Sending the smoke skyward
Beacons in the dusk,
Following on, silent and solitary
They plant a marching forest,
A war cemetery in miniature
White rabbit guards every six feet.
On the hillside a shallow grave
For young roots, tough and sinewy
Twisted and hairy, matted like mandrake
A badger skull unearthed, anointed
Pungent stubs of native garlic
Broken, bruised, consecrated with a toad.

'I am the resurrection and the life'
Sings the spade...'The life hereafter'
'Dust to dust. Bonfire ash to bonfire ash.'

Oak and sweet chestnut, beech and cherry
For ever and ever, the regeneration of timber.

V LAMBING

Already the flock has grown heavy
Bulbous and ponderous like boulders
They crowd out the feeding troughs,
The ewes broad and bulky in the beam
Fecund and fattening, they udder up
Move more slowly, cumbersome
Lie down and chew the cud
While shepherds delve into distant pockets
Hunt for the recalcitrant knife.

Pulling out pipes, they fasten hurdles
The inevitable barricade
Fishing with their eyes, dowsing
For some movement in the flock
Some stirring far underground
As if detecting a strange river
About to flood and burst its banks
Their stout hands poised and ready
At a moment's notice to draw the net in tight.

Suddenly one at a time
The ewes start to paw the ground
Turn and circle, go down
Smelling the straw, making a small nest.

Lips twitch, tongues dart,
Like a serpent mumbling
The breath different.
Up, round and then down again
Unusual noises, groaning a little.
With each breath, each push
Some ground is gained.
Straining, all the time straining
Neck to the sky, head to the heavens.

Restless they seek solitude
And then suddenly the waters break
Flowing down their flanks.
The neck arches once more and firm flesh opens
The thing slides down, wet and slimy in its sack
Catapulted, nose first towards the straw.

Like a dark seal it surfaces
Shudders a little, shakes its head
From side to side, shedding the veil
Ecstatic, chewing and nibbling
The proud ewe turns, mumbling to herself
Shunting the little beast into life.

Legs buckled, they stand and sway
Hunting and searching,
Awkward amidst the low slung wool.
Licked into shape hungry lambs
Connect at last, the feel of warmth
Dissolving in the mouth.
Bonded tightly to the swollen udder
Blood and milk mingle on the firm teat...

Out of the one come the two
An incorruptible message
Of what will live and what will die.
Blood earth and medicine,
Silently hanging between one world and another
The shepherd's art:
Invisible threads from a forgotten land.

Watching, all the time watching and waiting
As weeks drag on to months, the same adversary
Drags at your heels, the same furtive game
Curing the feeble pulse, lungs fight for air
Cold and shivering, the weak and dying
Brought in from the hedgerows.

Coaxed back into life, old ewes
Chew their last cud, ribs sunken and hollow.
Even before death, eyes are pecked out.
In gangs black and hooded, nature's terrorists
Pick off the stragglers one by one
While foxes wait till dusk.

Out of the one come the two
Coaxed and drawn, the swollen head
Winks at you, deformed and decayed
Aborted, the wet mouth, the watery belly
The orphan lamb adopted here and there
The second skin, like a dressing gown
Dragging on the ground, an overcoat
Smelling of rotten flesh.
Or else a prolapse, the breeding bag
Wantonly inside out, as if from outer space
The studs, the dark rosettes, black holes
Shuddering.
A wicked trifle two foot long
And a devil to get back on your own.
Amidst the straw:
Like dirty washing, spent afterbirth.
A spate of caesarians, the ewe stitched up.
Vet's instruments gleam in the moonlight.

Steady a little comes on the night watch
And then the flood before dawn
Urgent and fast like a tropical storm
Hot and steamy in the cold night air
The shepherd's hand dives deep
Into the watery cavern. Darkness folded tightly
Around the wrist, groping amidst the wet warmth
Fingers twist and turn, searching
For the head, congealed like seaweed
The slow tangle of feet, bent and unbent
Forelegs and backlegs, drawn gently and deftly
Through the tight noose of skin and muscle.

Exhausted by the long trance of her labour
The ewe yields up her last
And final quart of blood and water.
Turns and turns again, like a serpent mumbling.

Penned till dawn, the night's crop
Wait patient, ready for the first light
The moon's harvest ebbing at last,
High tide in the shepherd's eyes.
The shed quietens down
And the seething flock steadies itself.

Birds sing behind the barn
Sparrows and siskins visiting
Woodpeckers and pheasants
The welcome smell of bacon cooking.

Whoopee breakfast!

VI SILAGE

Keen see how the first leaves come out
Sticky buds, the tight knot unfurled
Keen see the banks come alive
The pulse quickens. Imagine how the seed must feel
Deep down, savouring that dark fertility
That small difference in warmth,
Seeking the light it cannot yet see
Thundering up to the sky.

And in one season, one season only
A crop, heady and prolific
The ingenious mechanism
Of roots spreading, patterns changing
Forming and dissolving
Repeats itself, time and time again.

Language without language
Ah. Yes...at long last
Something to talk about.

Orchids and bluebells, maggots and worms
Dose, dag, clip and trim
Chestnuts drip...a kestrel hovers.

Swallows and swifts come, stinging nettles too
And cuckoo spit. Careering round the lanes,
Milk tankers dash from farm to farm
Like anxious bees drowned in the heat of early summer.

Emerald green and bright in their first flush
Fields gleam and shine, rolled in their
Artificial stripes like school blazers,
Ready and waiting for the forage harvester,
Prehistoric beaks that ejaculate
The chopped grass skyward, into the backs of trailers
Sent rattling down the lanes,
Destined for the amphitheatre of old railway sleepers.

Slowly filled, stuffed and shiny
An enormous pillow, a bolster of black polythene
Anchored down by acres of old car tyres
Bare and bald, their journey long since over.
Slumbers vast and potent, solid and seeping
The silage clamp, a reservoir
Half forgotten till the autumn.
Warm and heady the workhouse gruel.

VII SHEARING

Fences are mended and lambs are weaned
The shepherd's job is never done
Flock upon flock is driven in
By keen eyed dogs, the unshorn tide
Hesitant and curious, devious and wary.

Peering over hedges, gangs of men
Listen to mutterings about the weather
A faint stirring, some mention of tackle
They oil the gear and hang the motors.
Every year the same curious dance
From farm to farm, the wandering skill
The knack of shearing sheep.

Penned and patient the ewes stand and pant
Yolk rising from the sticky belly
Are caught and turned, off guard
The delicate balance, poised and arched
The anxious minute, descending time and time again
The juddering handpiece, twisting and jiving
In long, seemingly easy strokes
Hugs the sheep's frame, swift and fluid
Deft and certain the arm's journey
Sweeps up and round, careful of eyes and ears
Udders and teats. Each man racing each other
The final curve, the back leg outstretched.

Over and over in sheaves of white and yellow
The fleece falls to the floor
Is gathered up in young girls' arms
Hugged like a lover, and then tossed down
Onto the tarpaulin, rolled tightly
And then stuffed into a bag
Sewn up and labelled, ready for the wool staplers.

Cold and startled, the ewes jump clear
Run back to their bleating. Stripped bare
They look boney, awkward, pruned
And liable to escape.

Swift, the haunting rhythm takes its toll.
In historic places we stretch the back
And quench the thirst.
Aching limbs seek the shade
Douse the heads in dirty troughs.

Sweat, dung and lanoline, the holy trinity
Ingrained in greasy trousers, sitting on wool sacks
We prise open sandwiches, the welcome smell
Of pipe tobacco, cider and scandal
The wry smile between gossip
As the farmer's daughter brings the tea.

In vain we try to make her blush
Half knowing her evening haunts.
A shapely figure she answers back
And holds her own, a farm hovering
About her shoulders, like an invisible shawl.

Magicians we move from flock to flock
Make ready for the Rams...

VIII SCYTHING

Gently we feel the edge of dawn creep forward
Between mist and pine.
Gently we swing the curved blade into the wet grass
Into the damp dew
Gently we edge knocked knees forward
Into the swathe.

Mowing ragwort and daisy
      smartweed and sorrell
      corncockle and chicory
Cutting, cutting, cutting close
Down to the roots, down to the moss
      timothy and foxtail
      charlock and dodder
      sweet vernal and sowthistle
Bowing to the rhythm of the scythe
The meadow's pasture, the measured stride
Creeping forward into the shadow's singing.

Swish   Swish   Swish   Swish

Home is where we come to
When we stop.
Searching and striving
These are foreigners then.

The password is no word at all.

Look at the stream and you will see the source:
Look at the source and you will see the ocean.

IX HARVEST

A time for hay and a time for harvest
A time for barley and a time for wheat
Shimmering just there in the midst
Of the all sucking heat, the silver sheen
Rippling in the breeze, just there
Over the hedge and behind the trees
Beyond the wide eyed cattle, flicking
Their fly ridden tails, and slobbery tongues.
Comes at last a dusty drone
Giant and subtropical, like an enormous locust
Gorging the corn mechanically
Bolting its food, sick with ladybirds
The golden stream pouring forth
Widgeon, Avalon, Marris Otter,
Huntsman, Galahad and Britannia,
Redstart and Apollo, Marinka and Natasha,
Poacher, Puffin and Dandy.

Carted and augered to fill the silos
Gently copulating with the sky.

While out the back, gleaming half-yellow
In serried ranks, comes the straw
Sullen acres of farmer's corduroy
Undulating and curvaceous
Heaped and humped.
Avenues ignited with a single match.

Racing and rioting, dusk and flames
Burst and burn, red stubble erupting
Inciting arson, dark figures armed
With pitch forks lift the fire here
And place it there, red and smutty
Silhouetted, sheets of flame
Soar and hang, as if the village
Were threatened, about to be burnt
As if vandals had suddenly emerged
From the hedgerows and fired the corn.

The farmer's secret vice.

Damp the shirts
Black the faces
Magnificent the sweat
Eerie the desolation.

In death as in life, they lean drunkenly
Swaying this way and that, the churchyard stones
Huddled, humped and jumbled.
'In Ever Loving Memory'
Wife on top of husband, husband on top of wife
One half of the village on top of the other half
Waiting 'Re-united' side by chilly side
Beneath the yew and monkey puzzle
Thoughts run wild, strange flickers of the eye
The odd unforgotten touch behind the barn
The gifts of flowers, strange fancies
Too close to home, when blood was thicker
Than water, and willing.
What strange conversations there must be
Buried deep, unspoken grief, longings
Lost daughters, children made men
And women borne and carried along
By the strong wind, entwined in the hedgerows
Footpaths still leading from back door to back door.
Whole families a fathom deep, the human harvest
Tucked up like potatoes in a resurrection clamp.

X GREAT WILTON

What am I bid?
What am I bid?   Cracking sheep these
                                 Healthy, wealthy sheep

Born on the downs
Not twenty miles away   What am I bid?
                                 What am I bid?

Come on gentlemen
Let's make it brisk   Thousands to sell
                                 What am I bid?

50 40 35
30 30 35
40 40 45   50
50 50 50   On my right
50 50 55   Lady's bid on the left
55   Cracking sheep these

Every one a goer
Two tooths   Look fine on your farm
All reared a lamb this year   Do I hear 60?
60 it is on my right   60 60 65
67.50   Lady's bid

Anyone advance?   Last chance
Make it snappy gentlemen   Do I have 70?
70 70 70   Madam your last bid
72½ 72½ 72½   Lady's bid on the left
All finished?   All finished?
I sell at 72½!

XI BURROW HILL CIDER FARM

Full circle stillness returns to the land
In fits and starts, acorns and beechnuts fall
Sheep are dipped and fat lambs sent for slaughter.

A time for drawing in and a time for gathering
A time for orchards and a time for cider.

There in the barn dark, layer by layer
Inch by inch, gallon by gallon
The steady inquisition begins
The confession extracted bit by bit
As the press pushes home, and the life blood
Of the heathen apple flows ever more freely
Till the stout cheese is dripping
Ruddy brown and golden like honey
A river in flood, a hive of fruit
Whole orchards, pulped and crushed
The never ending tide of trailers
Ebbing and flowing, acres deep and rounded
The mounds of apples, tipped and spewed forth
Like long barrows, the farmyard filled to bursting
Lagoons of red and yellow.

Brown Snout and Chisel Jersey
Dabinett and Porters' Perfection
Stoke Red and Kingston Black
Bloody Turk and Yarlington Mill
Lambrook Pippin and Tremlett's Bitter
Thom Putt and Royal Somerset.

Their ransomed juice pumped to distant vats
Vast in their yeast brooding
Potent and powerful, broad in the beam
Fecund and fattening, their froth fermenting bellies
Bound with oak and straps of iron
Barrels, giant and gargantuan.

A Norman trick this drink from apples
Distilled and fiery
A hint of orchard on the tongue.

Wind sun rain
What does it matter
To the man in the woods
When the year is drawing to an end.

> Leaves scatter—skies run
> Autumn wastes each wilder day.

The powerful breath of rams' tupping
The smell of hoof and horn
Impatient they stamp their feet.

> Imagine being jumped on
> From behind.
> That curious feeling
> Of entering life's chaos.

Rivers flood
Deer quiver
The earth smells of fox.

Time once more to return to the woods
Shabby jackets bound with binder twine
Alone and yet not alone, the wandering craft
The hidden skill, year in year out.

From forest to farmyard, from hedgerow to orchard
From flock to flock, the eyes and ears
Of the casual agricultural labourer.
Stubborn, diffuse, untidy, only a handful left.

These are the earth's true descendants
Who struggled to live, to stay alive
Learn from them before it is too late
The work of hands and generations of hands.

Old men shake their heads
And mutter under their breath.
To start and start again that is the secret.

Keen see how the sparhook dances
Glints like a fish in water
Scurrying upstream as it twists and turns
Canny and sure of its subtle purpose.

Hermitlike in the depths of the coppice
The same stout fingers begin once more
To weave their ancient tapestry
Coaxing and bending, till the cleft rods

Rift and ride, gleaming in curves
Like waves bucking and twisting
Through the silver bark of their flecked sea.
A hurdle empowered by calloused hands.

Pausing for a second, inquisitive and curious
Like a wild animal in the dappled light
The hurdlemaker listens to the coppice.
Charting the silence, gauging its depth.

And when no one is looking he slips the silence
Into the pocket of his battered tweed jacket
And takes it home, as you would
A rounded pebble that had caught your eye.

NOTES ON THE TEXT

These are intended to be a useful supplement and a source of
information in their own right. Wherever possible I have tried to
mention those people who in some way influenced my thinking and
with whom I worked closely. At times it is difficult to separate the
people from the land, and that is how it should be, places being
just as important and indeed more resilient than the human spirit,
but it is that spirit which over the years has transformed our landscape. Anyone who has broken in land, even in a small way, will
understand what I mean.

Unfortunately in the south of England so much land has now
been enclosed that few have any conception of what rough ground
looks like, or indeed what its spiritual importance is. I am always
thankful that the first sixteen years of my life were spent more or
less on the edge of Dartmoor, where at least man's efforts can be
seen in perspective and the true scale of life understood. Sheep
carcasses, granite tors, peat bogs and fast-flowing rivers have a
habit of making their presence felt.

But this work is concerned with more settled agriculture in the
softer regions, where farming is slightly more lucrative and the
larger farms more in need of extra labour. Only by going to the
third world can we truly understand the real importance of agriculture and its role in the transformation of human understanding.
What we have lost in the last hundred years is a deep respect for
the land, and it is this that I have tried to find and to share with
others within the writing.

HURDLEMAKING AND OLD MEN

A hurdle is in essence a lightweight moveable barricade to keep
sheep in or out, depending which way you look at it. Sadly, hurdle-
makers are on the decline, but their skill is well worth preserving.
The most difficult bit is splitting the hazel rods or gads as they are
sometimes called, without the sparhook running out. Inseparable
from shepherding, the two arts have always gone together. In 1793
John Claridge estimated that 15 dozen hurdles $4\frac{1}{2}$ feet long would
enclose an acre of ground and accommodate between 1200 and

1300 sheep. They were moved every morning. Not only did this process of folding keep sheep and lambs up together at night, but more importantly, their dung helped enormously to improve the yield of corn, and thus keep the fertility of the scant chalkland soils high. Vast tracts of Cranborne Chase woodlands were given over to coppicing. The rotation being about every seven or eight years, which was not only the average life of the hurdle but also the average life of a sheep, a simple and ingenious mechanism keeping many people employed during the winter months. Three or four acres being enough for one man in any given year. Even today hazel is still used for thatching spars and many still make them in their spare time. A sparhook is like a billhook but smaller and sharper, and better able to split the hazel. For a more comprehensive description of hurdlemaking see *Cranborne Chase* by Desmond Hawkins, pp124-127.

The hurdlemaker in the poem is Cecil Coombes of Ashmore, near Shaftesbury, with whom I worked on a number of occasions. He was a well known and jovial character who grew giant onions and sadly died suddenly in March 1987, collapsing in a hedge on his way back from the woods late one afternoon.

Rat's piss. Colloquial word for rough cider or scrumpy that has gone a bit over the top; usually cloudy and slightly vinegary.

Mizzling. Slang: to be cut off suddenly.

Dan dan. Outside lavatory, usually at the bottom of the garden. Dorset dialect, *dunnigan*.

As a matter of interest, minimum agricultural wages have now reached the princely sum of £3.32 an hour. Some get less & some get more, depending on whether they are casual or skilled. So the price of this book is equivalent to just over $2\frac{1}{2}$ hours farm work or $2\frac{1}{2}$ gallons of cider.

Often today we forget the enormous hardship and social change that occured not only with the Enclosure Acts but the emergence of a new type of farmer, who bought land rather than inherited it. It may well be that farming became more efficient, but for whom? Many farmworkers either died, fled to the towns, were transported

54

or simply emigrated. The plight of the landless labourers in the 18th and 19th centuries was appalling by any standards, and the worst in Europe. It was after all the reduction in wages from 9/- to 8/- a week which sparked off the actions of the Tolpuddle Martyrs in 1833. In their case, their wages went even lower—right down to 6/- a week, and this when wages in other parts of Dorset were 10/-.

For a more detailed look at present day farm wages, see the appendix at the end of the notes.

KITE HILL COPPICE

A ten acre wood near Durweston which I thinned with my brother in 1985-86. Mainly beech, it had like many other woodlands been planted after the war, and was receiving its first thinning in 35 years. Many of the forestry skills that I know were taught me by David Winskill of Iwerne Minster. It was with him that I worked for five years in West Wood near Compton Abbas Aerodrome.

Working tractors in the wet on steep slopes is particularly dangerous, and we were lucky not to have more injuries. Working on your own with a chainsaw miles from anywhere is also a sobering experience. As far as thinnings were concerned, we sold them as firewood. A cord of green beech weighing about two tons. A cord being a stack four by eight by four feet. *Cordwood* can also mean the top or lop wood from large trees that does not make timber. A Peugeot pickup load of logs was then worth about £30.

THE SMALL FARMER

Unfortunately, one of the side effects of the EEC system of farm subsidies & the necessary machinery specialisation that goes with it, has led to the decline of the small farmer. At one time 100 acres was a respectable size farm and many were half that size and able to support a family. Now a farm of 300 acres is barely sufficient to support three people and their families. More than anything it is the social change which has accompanied this that has radically altered the countryside, bringing with it artificially inflated land and house prices. Many farm labourers have been turned out of their tied cottages and may be self-employed or living in council houses. The maximisation of farming techniques was relevant during the war at the height of the U-boat campaign, but its scientific and chemical extension into the 80s and 90s has left more unsolved problems than farmer's incomes. It may well be that smaller farms will once more become viable, if they can specialise and diversify in a way that is sympathetic to the environment.

For some, farming is only a tax loss to be offset against other income, a useful entrée into the world of shooting, hunting and local politics. A way of entertaining your friends. I always find it amusing that there is only one letter different in pheasant from peasant.

Attitudes to hunting and shooting vary as do the attitudes to farming, but if the hunter were hunted a little more often then things would be more in perspective. When they have to dig big pits just to bury the pheasants, you begin to wonder what it is all about. It is however time perhaps that the voice and concerns of the small farmer were heard more readily, before all the small farms are gobbled up.

Slurry is the semi-liquid deposit left behind by cows, usually after housing them in the yard before and after milking. This is then swept up into the slurry pit, which itself is periodically emptied.

TREE PLANTING

This is often done in the winter months while the ground is not frozen or waterlogged. Rabbit guards and plastic tubes to prevent damage from deer are commonplace and ensure a better survival rate. Undergrowth is always a problem and the labour required in keeping a young plantation in order can be enormous. Unfortunately, many of the softwood plantations, unless they are of high quality, are uneconomic to thin until they are twenty or thirty years old. Luckily the government has begun to close the tax loopholes that encouraged the mass planting of softwoods. Paradoxically many of our finest woodlands were laid out between 100 and 200 years ago, specifically with shooting in mind.

56

LAMBING

This is always the best time on the farm, if it goes well. The hours are long and the vexations endless. Night shepherds are a special breed, preferring their own isolation and responsibility to the hurly-burly of the day shift. Very often they are left on their own with anything up to 1500 sheep. Lambing, like shearing, cannot really be taught, so much of it is experience and intuition.

One person in particular who helped me was Anne Hodgson of Ashmore. Now in her seventies, she enjoys the quiet life, but kept sheep until three years ago and did night lambing on large estates.

The lambing described here could be anywhere, but this particular flock was outside Shaftesbury. The shepherd was Walt Pitman and the owner John Eliot Gardiner.

Wet mouth is nearly always fatal. It is caused by E.Coli.

Watery belly is a well known condition at birth where the belly is abnormally swollen, and may be linked to abortion virus.

Orphan lambs are often adopted by skinning a dead lamb and then dressing the orphan up in the skin to make another mother accept it. After a few days it takes on an aroma all of its own.

SILAGE

This often clashes with shearing & has largely replaced haymaking which was always a risky business at the best of times. One farmer near Shaftesbury actually hung himself after a bad crop. Sometimes I have been employed all day simply burning black soggy bales. The advantage of silage is that you can get several cuts, but it needs a fair bit of 'artificial' to bring it on. If made well it has a higher feed value and is often fed to sheep as well as cattle. Large clamps, if fed on the open face principle, can be dangerous, and in several instances men and cattle have been killed by avalanches of silage. Farming is in fact one of the most dangerous occupations, partly because of its isolation, and partly because of the machinery involved. It is second only to mining and fishing. Last year sixty-three people were killed in the UK in farming related accidents. Eleven were in the South West.

Dose refers to worming sheep or drenching them.

Dag refers to cutting the shitty bits off the sheep's back end to prevent flystrike or maggots, which in the summer are the larvae of greenbottle. Sheep ought to be crutched out twice a year.

Clip and trim refers to foot paring which is a dirty job like dagging. The shepherd trims off the unwanted hoof, which these days have a tendency to grow quite fast, as few flocks are ever driven on the roads or in droves.

SHEARING

After lambing this is a swift operation. New Zealanders can shear up to 300 a day. If I do half that number I am a happy man, but it is not an easy skill to learn, and requires a fair degree of commitment and tolerance to pain. I learnt first, hand shearing in the Outer Hebrides, and then worked for a contractor called Jim Dickens who taught both my brother and myself the old English way, where you go down one side, do the belly and then the other side. Much simpler than the Kiwi method, and much easier to hold the sheep. To be sure the Kiwi method is faster and better for small sheep and lambs, but for big rams and Dorset Horn ewes I much prefer the old way.

The secret of shearing is in the rhythm and in not getting flustered, combined with sharp gear, a strong back and an efficient catching system. Some farms are so ramshackle you wonder how they make a living at all. Some still don't even have electricity.

As for economics, shearing, like wool, has taken a nose dive in real terms. In 1981 the guaranteed guide price for wool was 115p per kilo or about 50p per pound. Shearing was about 50p, as was a pint of beer. By 1985 the price of wool had crept up to 129p per kilo where it stayed for 5 years. In 1990 it fell to 125p & farmers only got 85% of that. In 1991 the price dropped again to 120p and farmers are only getting 50% of that, the rest payable later if it sells. So in fact after ten years the price of wool has only risen 5p per kilo, the average fleece being about 2-3 kilos, though some are much heavier. The world wool price has fallen dramatically and the outlook for the Wool Board and the farmer alike is not good. As for shearing on large flocks, I get only 60-65p, which will just buy you half a pint of beer at today's prices. So in fact we are doing the same work, blood sweat and tears, for effectively half what we were ten years ago. Working for a shearing contractor I would be lucky to get 35p per sheep. One shearer I spoke to in Devon said that when he started it was 2/6 for shearing and 2/6 for a haircut. Today you are lucky to get a haircut for less than £2.

The EEC system of subsidies and grants may have benefited the farmer, but it has turned farmers into agri-business men, and the benefits are rarely if ever passed on to the workers in the same proportions. Shearers only survive by shearing large numbers of sheep, crippling their backs, and heading off to the pub. Many retire before they are thirty.

One man in Dorset, Norman Strawbridge, who sharpens my gear, was still shearing 100 a day at the age of 63, and only gave up because he fell off a timber lorry and injured his arm. It is perhaps better to shear fewer, but keep shearing for longer.

SCYTHING

Even after the reaper and binder made its appearance at the turn of the century, a man would still be sent out to cut the first swathe and open up the field around the hedges and gateways. A thirsty job at the best of times, and like shearing and sparhooks, the secret was in the sharpness and in the method of sharpening.

Best to start early in the morning before the sun gets too high. No wonder so much cider was drunk.

HARVEST

Combined harvesters came to Britain in the late thirties. At the outbreak of war in 1939 there were 46 of them. They gradually replaced the reaper binder which today is only really used by those growing thatching straw, which can fetch as much as £400 a ton. Working on a thrashing machine or reed comber was long, dusty and relentless work. Ricks are still made in some places and the tackle dragged from farm to farm. Straw that has had too much 'artificial' and straw retarders in it is of course useless, and only the old varieties will do. More than a few corn dolly makers have bemoaned the EEC short straw. The main advantage of combined harvesters is of course their speed and the fact that they can do in a day what would take a gang of men several weeks, and this in fact means that the farmer is less at the mercy of the weather than in times past.

Straw burning is more or less obsolete now, and even stubble burning is on the way out, but a field on fire used to be quite a sight. People are in a sense a harvest as well, and it is no coincidence that Death wields a scythe. The best churchyards are however grazed with sheep.

Straw can of course be used for bedding, feed and for building cob walls, an art still known in Devon. Planners take note for good cheap housing: there is nothing better than a well thatched cob house, and many are still standing after hundreds of years. Of the corn varieties mentioned, only Widgeon and Huntsman give long straw suitable for thatching.

GREAT WILTON

One of the largest sheep fairs in the south. Usually they occur in the first weeks of August, September, October and November, the largest by far being September, selling around 30,000 ewes, lambs and pedigree rams. Hurdles are much in evidence. The sale starts with a man ringing a big hand bell. A good sheep sale brings everyone out of the woodwork.
Two tooths refers to young sheep who only have two teeth up. Some like them to have had a lamb, some don't. *GTU* means good on tooth and udder, applicable to older sheep in case they have had mastitis or lost all their teeth.

BURROW HILL CIDER FARM

Owned and run by Julian and Di Temperley. Not only does it make some of the best cider in the South West, which has won

many prizes, but they have between them almost singlehandedly
pioneered the production of cider brandy on a commercial scale,
producing a smooth full flavour as good as any Calvados in France.
It comes off the still at 70% proof and is aged in various types of
oak cask. The French in Normandy have been particularly helpful
and the two stills, which came from there, are called Josephine and
Fifi, and have their own Gallic temperaments. Josephine is solid
and reliable, Fifi is small and fast. The spirit is brought down to
42% in easy stages and should be available from September 1991.
The cider farm is situated near Kingsbury Episcopi in Somerset.
A *cheese* is the stack of pomace ready to go into the press, usually
14-16 layers, each layer wrapped in a cloth.
Pomace is the pulp of crushed apples which, when spent is fed to
sheep and cattle, or spread on the land.

There are hundreds of varieties of cider apples, but the real
tragedy is that people are not replanting orchards, and this because
of cheap imported apple concentrate from abroad. Good farmhouse
cider is the cheapest and most sensible drink of all. Still only 72p
a pint in some pubs when commercial fizzy cider is £1.20. The
problem is that many pubs are owned by large breweries who hate
cider, so they put the price up to the same level as beer, which is
not exactly in their customers' best interests.
Fat lamb refers to lamb that is up to weight, usually 80-100 lbs,
and to be graded has to be lean not fat. Other lambs are sold as
stores, to be fattened up by somebody else.

THE SMELL OF HOOF AND HORN

Rams tupping: creation when all else is dying or falling. Sheep
are, I believe, at their most fertile on the shortest day of the year.
The gestation period for a sheep is about five months or 150 days.
Put the ram in on Guy Fawkes night and they come out on April
Fool's day. That ensures that the lambs will appear as the first
flush of grass is coming through to boost the ewe's milk. The sight
of a large flock with lambs in an orchard at blossom time is not
without its attractions even for the grumpiest farmer.

APPENDIX

	Min. agricultural wages per hour	per week	Lambing per night	Shearing per 100	Wool per kilo	Beer per pint
1981	£1.60	£64	£30	£50	£1.15	50p
1982	£1.76	£70.40	£30	£50	£1.15	52p
1983	£1.89	£75.40	£35	£55	£1.15	54p
1983	£1.98	£79.20	£35	£55	£1.15	60p
1984	£2.07	£82.80	£36	£55	£1.20	64p
1985	£2.24	£89.70	£36	£55	£1.29	66p
1986	£2.36	£94.45	£40	£60	£1.29	70p
1987	£2.48	£99.20	£40	£60	£1.29	75p
1988	£2.60	£104.20	£42	£60	£1.29	80p
1989	£2.80	£112.02	£42	£65	£1.29	90p
1990	£3.05	£122.10	£48	£70	£1.25	£1
1991	£3.32	£129.43	£50	£70	£1.20	£1.20
Rises	107%	107%	66%	40%	4%	140%

In these days of massive wage increases for top management, these figures speak for themselves.

The average rate for normal self-employed farm labour is about £1 more per hour than the minimum, but then self-employed labourers often have to travel twenty or more miles to a job, they have the cost of their equipment, they have no house provided, no overtime, no paid holidays, and they have no job security whatsoever, as well as paying their own National Insurance.

A night shift lambing is twelve hours on, twelve hours off, seven days a week, sometimes for six or eight weeks on the trot. At the moment I help lamb one flock of 500 near Montacute and another of 1300 near Marlborough, which, when you are on your own at night, is quite enough to be getting on with. And all this for £4 an hour. It is however the way of life and freedom of movement which is the attraction.

Enough said about wool, but things may get worse, which is ironic for a product that was at the very centre of the economy for at least five hundred years, and gave the wealth needed for some of our most important architecture. The rates for shearing have not risen very much—many New Zealanders only get 35p per sheep from the contractors. In comparison with minimum agricultural wages, in 1981 a shearer had to shear 128 sheep to get the equivalent of a week's wage; now he has to shear 185, an increase of 44%.

As far as beer is concerned, the increases are not only dramatic but iniquitous. It is after all the farmers who grow the malting barley in the first place. By contrast, Burrow Hill dry cider at the farm gate is now £3.00 a gallon or 38p per pint. The cider brandy is about £16 a bottle, which when you consider that the conversion ratio is nearly 10:1 is not bad at all.

To an outsider these figures and comparisons may not seem important, but the trend is clear. Self-employed hard-sweated and skilled farm labour is on the decline and the trends would appear to work to the farmer's advantage, but the price they are getting for their products is also falling. Times may get worse, but spare a thought for the casual labourer. Every generation they work hard and leave little except the landscape, and that is their inheritance, which is why in a sense they merge into it. Without landscape where would literature or the English language be?

What concerns me however is that farming may come to be seen as a subsidised ecological leisure industry, when in fact it is the source of all things. You are what you eat. Or as Mr Buttress, an old farmer near Shaftesbury once said to me as we were shearing his sheep, 'Agriculture is the tree of life....and industry only its branches'. Tinker with the roots and you affect the leaves. Perhaps it was no coincidence that some of the first inventions of the Industrial Revolution were to do with the manufacture of wool. Another equally valid observation came from an old woman called Mrs Bowden, who used to live next to my grandparents in Meavy on the edge of Dartmoor. When she was well into her nineties, I asked her about changes in the village and her reply has stuck with me ever since. 'The trouble with villages these days' she said, 'is that people aren't themselves any more'. How right she is.

Blood Earth & Medicine is set in 11 and 14 point
Monotype Series 101 Imprint, and was printed during
September 1991 at the Parrett Press, Martock.
It was bound by West Country Binders & Print
Finishers Ltd of Weston-Super-Mare.
The text paper is 90 gsm Elan book wove, and the
cover paper 130 gsm Hahnemühle Bugra Bütten.
The Heidelberg cylinder printing machine used, was
previously owned by the author's brother, who saved
it from the jaws of the breakers in 1980.